W9-CDV-716

WINGS

Birds, bees, biplanes, and other things with wings

Words by Tracey Turner   Art by Fatti Burke

For Meg, Monty, and Wellington

WINGS

Birds, bees, biplanes, and other things with wings

Words by Tracey Turner   **Art by Fatti Burke**

KINGFISHER
LONDON & NEW YORK

A Raspberry Book
Editorial: Kath Jewitt
Art direction: Sidonie Beresford-Browne
Cover design: Sidonie Beresford-Browne
Internal design: Peter Clayman
Consultant: Jack Challoner

KINGFISHER
LONDON & NEW YORK

Text and design copyright © Raspberry Books Ltd 2020
First published 2020 in the United States by Kingfisher,
120 Broadway, New York, NY 10271
Kingfisher is an imprint of
Macmillan Children's Books, London
All rights reserved.

Distributed in the U.S. and Canada by Macmillan,
120 Broadway, New York, NY 10271

Library of Congress Cataloging-in-Publication Data has been applied for.

ISBN: 978-0-7534-7553-9

Kingfisher books are available for special promotions and premiums.
For details contact: Special Markets Department, Macmillan, 120 Broadway,
New York, NY 10271

For more information, please visit
www.kingfisherbooks.com

Printed in China
1 3 5 7 9 8 6 4 2
1TR/0520/UG/WKT/128MA

Contents

I'm the fastest-flying bird—you can't catch me!

Introduction

Wings first appeared on Earth far back in the mists of time. Since then, they've proved to be very useful indeed. Insects, pterosaurs, birds, and bats all swooped through the skies millions of years before people figured out how to use wings. In fact, people dreamed about flying, and made up stories about it, long before they discovered how to do it.

As well as our feathered, furry, and six-legged flying friends, you'll find out about winged horses, unicorns, and dragons; biplanes, helicopters, and solar-powered planes; and courageous flying monks.

So clamber into the cockpit of your supersonic plane, or strap on a wingsuit and climb a mountain if you'd rather, and come for a fascinating flight. It's time to discover the wonder of wings.

Fly in the Wright brothers' biplane.

Discover some of the most extraordinary and unusual wings in the world!

Find out about a flying reptile the size of a giraffe.

How Wings Work

Birds and bats use their strong muscles to flap their wings, pushing them forward through the air. As the animals move along at high speed, the air moving above and below the wings creates an upward force called lift.

The lift force pushes the animals up, and keeps them in the air. Airplane wings work in the same way, but airplanes have propellers or jet engines that push them forward through the air, instead of muscles.

Flying Insects

Hundreds of millions of years ago, insects were the first creatures ever to fly on planet Earth.

Today there are more insects than any other type of creature in the world— around 900,000 different kinds that we know of. Scientists think there are about a billion insects for every human!

The soft back wings are for flying.

A beetle's front wings are made of hard material and protect the back wings.

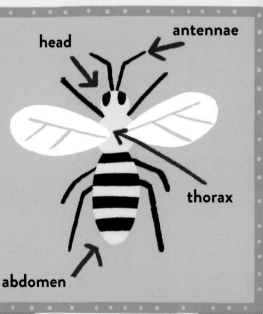

When they close, the back wings fold up like a clever origami paper model.

Insect Wings

Insects are animals with two feelers (or antennae), six legs, and a body made up of three parts (head, thorax, and abdomen). Not all of them can fly. Most flying insects have two sets of wings, but some, including flies, have only one set. Flies often have rods on the sides of their bodies that help keep them steady as they fly, instead of a second set of wings.

head

antennae

thorax

abdomen

I'm a beetle. I have two sets of wings, which you can see when I open them to fly.

Insects fly at different speeds. The fastest are dragonflies, which can zip along at more than 30 miles per hour (50 km/h). Flies are slower, but they're aerial acrobats—they can hover, and fly backward and sideways, like helicopters.

Dragonfly

Lots of insects make a buzzing sound because their wingbeats make the air around them vibrate.

I beat my wings at 200 times a second. **Bzzzzzzzzzz**

That's nothing! Midges like me can beat our wings more than a thousand times a second! Bzzzzzzzzzz

Midge

Bee

Butterflies

These gorgeous creatures have some of the world's most beautiful wings. The biggest butterfly—and perhaps the most gorgeous of all—is Queen Alexandra's birdwing butterfly.

The male Queen Alexandra's birdwing doesn't grow nearly as big as the female but makes up for it with a bright yellow body and electric-blue-and-aquamarine-colored wings. Female Queen Alexandra's birdwings can have wingspans of up to 11 inches (28 cm), but, to be honest, they're a bit drab by comparison.

Butterflies are found in most parts of the world, but all the ones you can see here are from tropical rain forests.

Butterfly Magic

Butterflies attach their eggs to leaves with a gluey substance. Each egg hatches into a caterpillar, which grows and grows, and then turns into a pupa with a hard case around it called a chrysalis. In one of the natural world's most spectacular magic tricks, the pupa changes inside the chrysalis, growing wings and emerging as an adult butterfly.

This male Queen Alexandra's birdwing measures 7.5 inches (19 cm) across—they can reach this size in real life.

Sadly, Queen Alexandra's birdwings are an endangered species. They live only in the rain forest of Papua New Guinea, and they are very fussy. They only lay their eggs on plants called aristolochias, which are also the only plants they feed on. The caterpillars eat the plant, which makes them taste horrible to predators, and the adult butterflies sip the plant's nectar.

Butterflies smell with their antennae, and taste with their feet as well as with their mouths. A butterfly's mouth is a long, strawlike proboscis, which uncurls to suck up nectar or juice from plants.

Flying Reptiles

Flying reptiles swooped across prehistoric skies in the age of the dinosaurs, millions of years before birds and bats. They were the biggest flying creatures in the history of the world.

There were lots of different kinds of pterosaur. Some were only the size of sparrows and flitted through prehistoric forests snapping up insects. This Anhanguera had sharp, snarly teeth for catching and keeping hold of fish, and a crest on its snout.

I'm only 30 inches (76 cm) tall, but my wings are **16.5 feet (5 m) across!**

Flying reptiles—or pterosaurs—were around for a very long time. They first appeared about 225 million years ago, and died out completely about 66 million years ago, at the same time as the dinosaurs disappeared.

The First Birds

Birds weren't the first things to fly, but once they got going they became really good at it. They've been flapping around for many millions of years.

All birds alive today are the descendants of a particular group of meat-eating feathered dinosaurs. Archaeopteryx was a funny looking cross between a dinosaur and a bird. It lived at the end of the Jurassic period, around 147 million years ago.

Who are you calling funny looking?

Archaeopteryx wasn't very big—its fossils vary in size between a magpie and a chicken. Instead of a beak it had jaws with teeth, feathered arms, and a long, bony, feathery tail. No one knows for sure, but it probably couldn't fly very far—just in short flappy bursts, a bit like a modern chicken.

Long after Archaeopteryx, birds much more like modern ones took flight around 70 million years ago, during the Cretaceous Period. Compared to Archaeopteryx, their bones were much lighter and thinner and their feathers were longer. Their arms had turned into wings much longer than their legs, and their tails had become short and feathered too.

I'm Ichthyornis, from the Cretaceous Period. I'm a fish-eating sea bird with teeth!

Us kairuku penguins were even taller than emperor penguins.

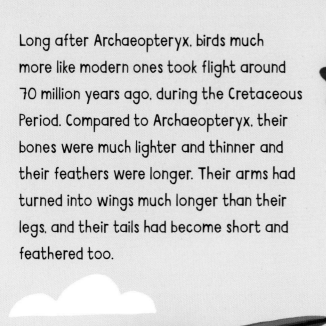

Flightless birds have been around a long time, too. Kairuku penguins lived around 50 million years ago. Like modern penguins they stood upright and waddled around, but they weren't such good swimmers as penguins are today.

Lots of Birds

Today there are thousands of different kinds of birds. All of them have feathers, but their wings are different shapes to suit how they fly.

Small woodland birds fly between trees, so they need to swerve around, and to stop and take off quickly. Their stubby, broad wings are the best shape for that kind of skillful flying.

Three Feathers

Birds have long, stiff wing feathers to help them fly, and tail feathers to help them steer in the sky. Wing feathers are pointed and tail feathers are more rounded on the tip. Birds also have small, fluffy body feathers to help keep them warm.

Rounded tail feather

Downy body feather

Pointed wing feather

I just need to dodge around this tree and grab that beetle . . .

I'm really high up, but I can still spot prey with my eagle eyes.

Eagles and other birds of prey need to soar high above the ground. To help them do this they have long, wide wings tipped with feathers that are separated like fingers.

Birds that make long journeys need wings to help them go fast through the air. Ducks and swallows have these high-speed wings, which are long and slightly bent.

I have to be **super-fast** to catch insects.

Swallow

Seabirds, such as seagulls, have long, narrow wings to help them glide along. They ride the winds effortlessly with their wings outstretched.

Bats

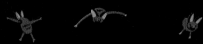

These furry, leathery-winged creatures are the world's only flying mammals, and some of its most amazing animals.

Most of the world's bats swoop around eating insects at night. By day, they roost in dark, out-of-the-way places, such as inside caves and under bridges. This means they keep away from daytime predators and take advantage of tasty nighttime insects.

There are over 1,200 different kinds of bats . . .

. . . that's nearly one fifth of all the world's species of mammal.

Among all the hundreds of different types of bats, there are some very unusual ones. Caribbean white tent bats are little balls of white fluff with yellow ears and a yellow nose. They nibble on rain forest leaves and fold them up to make a tent to roost in during the day.

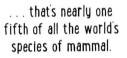

Bat Wings

A bat's wing is like a human arm and hand with skin stretched between the bones. The part that would be a thumb on a human hand is a little claw sticking out of the bat's wing, so it can crawl and climb.

I'm just nuts about **fruit!**

Many bats use echolocation to find their way in the dark. They make high-pitched sounds, then listen to the echoes as the sound bounces back to build up a picture of what's around them. Fruit bats use their lovely big eyes instead. These whoppers can get much bigger than their smaller relatives—one of the largest is the golden-crowned flying fox, which has a wingspan of up to 5.5 feet (1.7 m)!

5.5 feet (1.7 m)

Magical Wings

Plenty of real animals have wings. But there are stories of magical winged creatures, including flying horses and fire birds.

What on earth . . .

The tale of the phoenix bird has been told since Ancient Egyptian times. The story goes that the phoenix lives for 1,000 years, then builds a nest and sings a song so perfect that even the Sun stops to listen. A spark falls from the Sun and sets fire to the bird in the nest, but a new phoenix is reborn from the ashes to live for the next 1,000 years.

Chinese dragons are said to look after the world and bring good luck. They are made up of lots of different animals, including the head of a camel, the body of a snake, and the claws of a hawk. Yinglong the mythical rain dragon has wings, too. He's said to control the rain and he can stop rivers from flooding with his tail.

Pegasus is a famous flying horse in an Ancient Greek myth. The hero Bellerophon captured and tamed Pegasus, and together they flew off to fight a monster called the chimera, who was part lion, part goat, and part dragon. Later, Zeus, the king of the gods, turned Pegasus into a constellation of stars in the northern sky.

Griffins often appear on carvings and badges around royal palaces and castles in Europe. They are part lion and part eagle—the lion is said to be king of the animals, and the eagle is said to be king of the birds.

Flying unicorns are called alicorns. The first ones we know of were shown on carvings in Ancient Assyria (the region we now call Iraq) around 2,500 years ago.

21

The Flight of Icarus

Watch out Icarus, your wings are made of **wax!**

A long time before there were flying machines, or even kites, people dreamed of flying and made up stories about it. The story of Icarus was first told more than 2,000 years ago in Ancient Greece.

The story of Icarus

Long ago, on the island of Crete, King Minos had a monster problem: the Minotaur— half bull, half man—had to be kept under control. King Minos asked an inventor named Daedalus for help. Daedalus built the labyrinth, an underground maze that was so cleverly designed that no one could find their way around it. King Minos imprisoned the Minotaur inside the labyrinth (but that's another story).

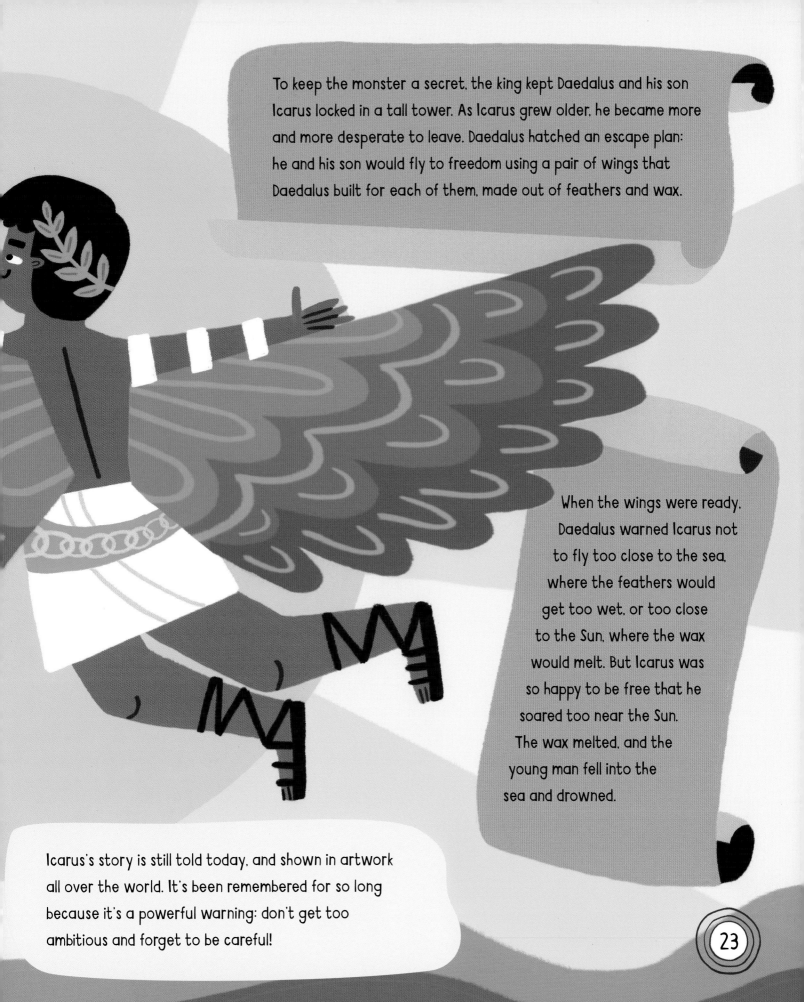

To keep the monster a secret, the king kept Daedalus and his son Icarus locked in a tall tower. As Icarus grew older, he became more and more desperate to leave. Daedalus hatched an escape plan: he and his son would fly to freedom using a pair of wings that Daedalus built for each of them, made out of feathers and wax.

When the wings were ready, Daedalus warned Icarus not to fly too close to the sea, where the feathers would get too wet, or too close to the Sun, where the wax would melt. But Icarus was so happy to be free that he soared too near the Sun. The wax melted, and the young man fell into the sea and drowned.

Icarus's story is still told today, and shown in artwork all over the world. It's been remembered for so long because it's a powerful warning: don't get too ambitious and forget to be careful!

People Take Off!

People have been fascinated by flight for thousands of years—after all, birds make it look so easy. Before the invention of planes, we tried all sorts of ways to get airborne.

Like Icarus in the Greek myth, some people made wings like birds' wings, complete with feathers, attached them to their arms, and jumped off tall buildings. The results were short, fast, and often painful. One of the flyers was a monk named Eilmer of Malmesbury in the 11th century.

You can do it **Eilmer!**

Artist, scientist, and all-around genius Leonardo da Vinci was interested in flying. He drew more than 100 designs for flying machines, but he didn't build one as far as we know—at least, not a successful one.

In China, people had been flying kites since about 400 BC, and people tried to fly using kites for centuries afterward. Some were successful, but gliders proved much better—find out more about them on the next page. Kites were also used to test the strength of the wind, send messages, and measure distances—and just for fun.

People managed to get properly airborne for the first time in 1783, when the first hot air balloon went up. But it took a bit longer for flying machines with wings.

Gliders

Gliders were the first aircraft that weren't lighter than air, like balloons. Now people really were flying.

An inventor named George Cayley built the first successful glider in 1853. Cayley was 79 years old by that time, so one of his household servants flew it. Cayley was also the first person to have the idea for the design of the modern airplane, though he didn't make one. He invented lots of other things too, like caterpillar tracks and seatbelts.

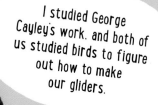

I studied George Cayley's work, and both of us studied birds to figure out how to make our gliders.

Otto Lilienthal built even better gliders in the 1890s. To launch them, he jumped into the wind from somewhere high—he even built an artificial hill for the purpose. Altogether, he made around 2,000 flights. Sadly, he had an accident on one flight, and died the next day.

Modern hang gliders are more like Otto Lilienthal's gliders—a big wing made out of a simple frame covered in fabric. The pilot hangs in a harness underneath the wing, and, like Lilienthal, runs downhill into the wind to launch, then glides on warm air currents.

Wheeeeee

Today's gliders don't look much like Cayley's or Lilienthal's, but they can stay in the air for hours rather than a few minutes. They have to be towed by a plane to get airborne, or hoisted up on a long cable attached to a car or a winch.

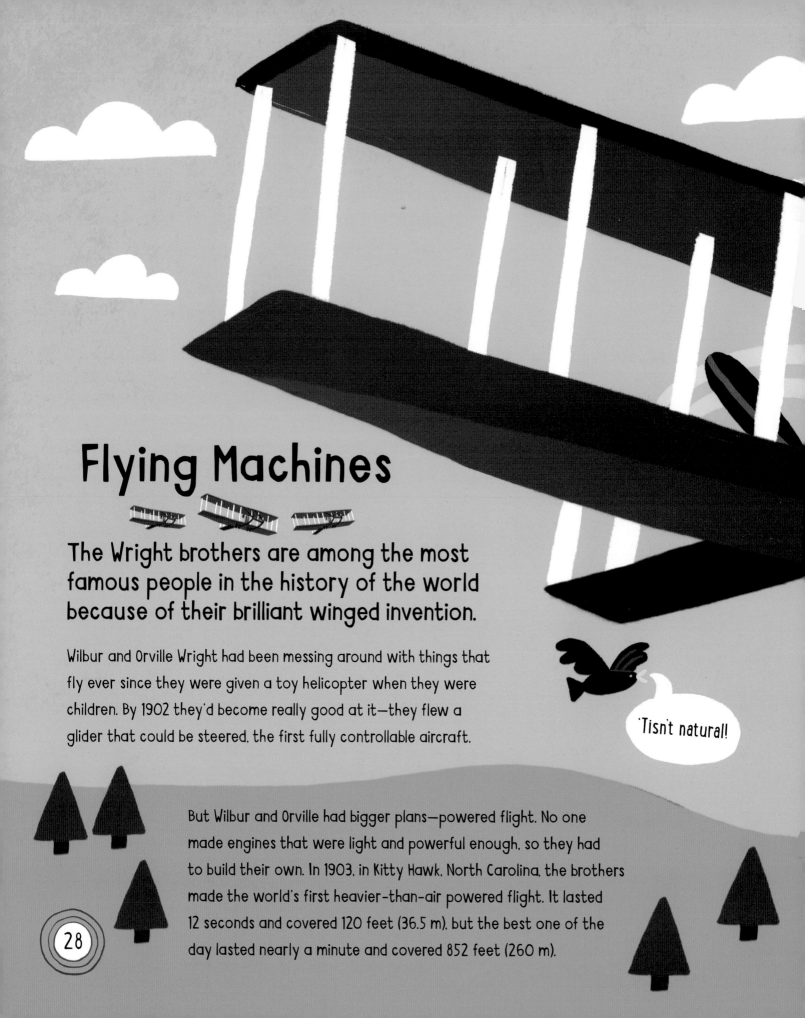

Flying Machines

The Wright brothers are among the most famous people in the history of the world because of their brilliant winged invention.

Wilbur and Orville Wright had been messing around with things that fly ever since they were given a toy helicopter when they were children. By 1902 they'd become really good at it—they flew a glider that could be steered, the first fully controllable aircraft.

'Tisn't natural!

But Wilbur and Orville had bigger plans—powered flight. No one made engines that were light and powerful enough, so they had to build their own. In 1903, in Kitty Hawk, North Carolina, the brothers made the world's first heavier-than-air powered flight. It lasted 12 seconds and covered 120 feet (36.5 m), but the best one of the day lasted nearly a minute and covered 852 feet (260 m).

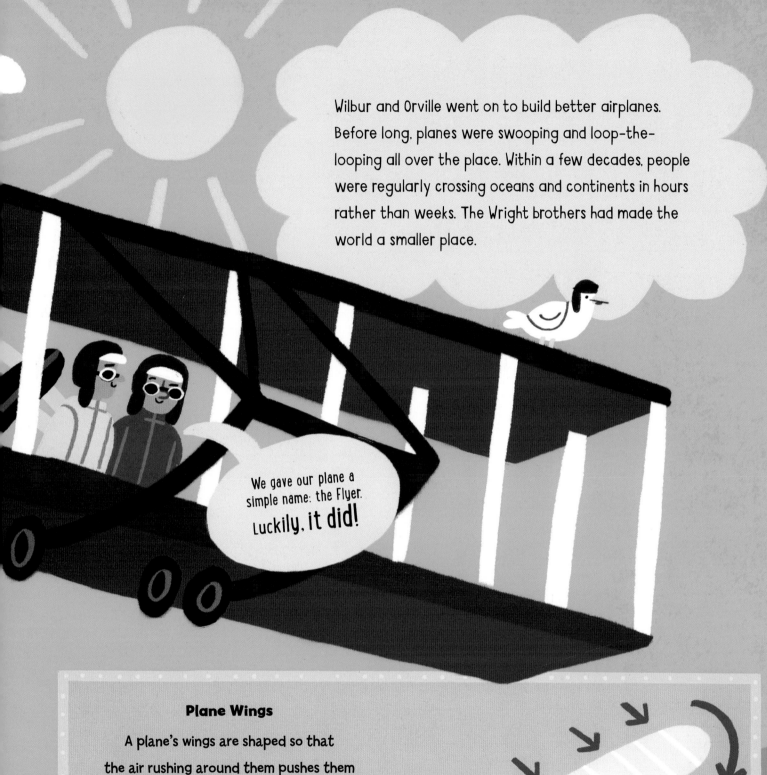

Wilbur and Orville went on to build better airplanes. Before long, planes were swooping and loop-the-looping all over the place. Within a few decades, people were regularly crossing oceans and continents in hours rather than weeks. The Wright brothers had made the world a smaller place.

We gave our plane a simple name: the Flyer. Luckily, it did!

Plane Wings

A plane's wings are shaped so that the air rushing around them pushes them upward into the sky. The Wright Flyer, and other early planes, were biplanes, with two sets of wings. These gave the planes a big wing area —useful because early engines weren't very powerful—and a sturdy structure.

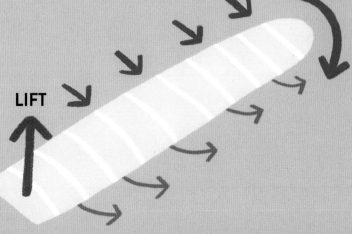

LIFT

From Biplanes to Supersonic Planes

My plane was called the Spirit of St. Louis.

After Wilbur and Orville Wright's biplane took off, it was quite a short flight to today's supersonic computerized aircraft.

In the early 1900s people entered flying competitions, which offered cash prizes for new flying records. The most famous winner was American Charles Lindbergh, who became the first person to fly the Atlantic solo and nonstop in 1927.

The first passenger-carrying jet plane was developed in the late 1940s and entered service in 1952. In those days it was an unusual way to travel. Now millions of people use jet planes every year.

In 1947 U.S. pilot Chuck Yeager flew his Bell X-1 rocket plane at supersonic speed—faster than the speed of sound—for the first time. When a plane passes the speed of sound, sudden air changes around it cause a booming noise called a sonic boom.

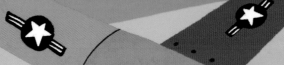

The faster the better!

In 1939 the world's first jet plane, the Heinkel 178, flew for the first time. In a jet engine, air is sucked in at the front and squeezed into a chamber, where it's mixed with fuel and set alight to make the plane move really fast.

More than 100,000 flights take off every day! We need to invent an environmentally friendly plane . . .

Most modern passenger and cargo planes are controlled by onboard computers called autopilot. The real pilot is still needed for takeoff and landing though, and in case something goes wrong.

Concorde was a supersonic passenger plane that flew from 1976 until 2003. It could fly at more than 1,300 miles per hour (2,090 km/h)!

Planes of the Future

We rely on planes to transport all sorts of things, from vacationers to frozen fish. But most planes need aviation fuel to fly, which contributes to pollution and global warming. We need to find environmentally friendly ways to fly.

Solar-powered planes use the Sun to charge their batteries. In 2016 Bertrand Piccard and André Borschberg completed the first around-the-world flight using solar power, in their plane Solar Impulse 2.

U.S. space agency NASA is one of the organizations that is working hard to make planes that use electric motors instead of aviation fuel. Although electrically powered model aircraft have been around for decades, it's proving a lot harder to build a full-size electric plane.

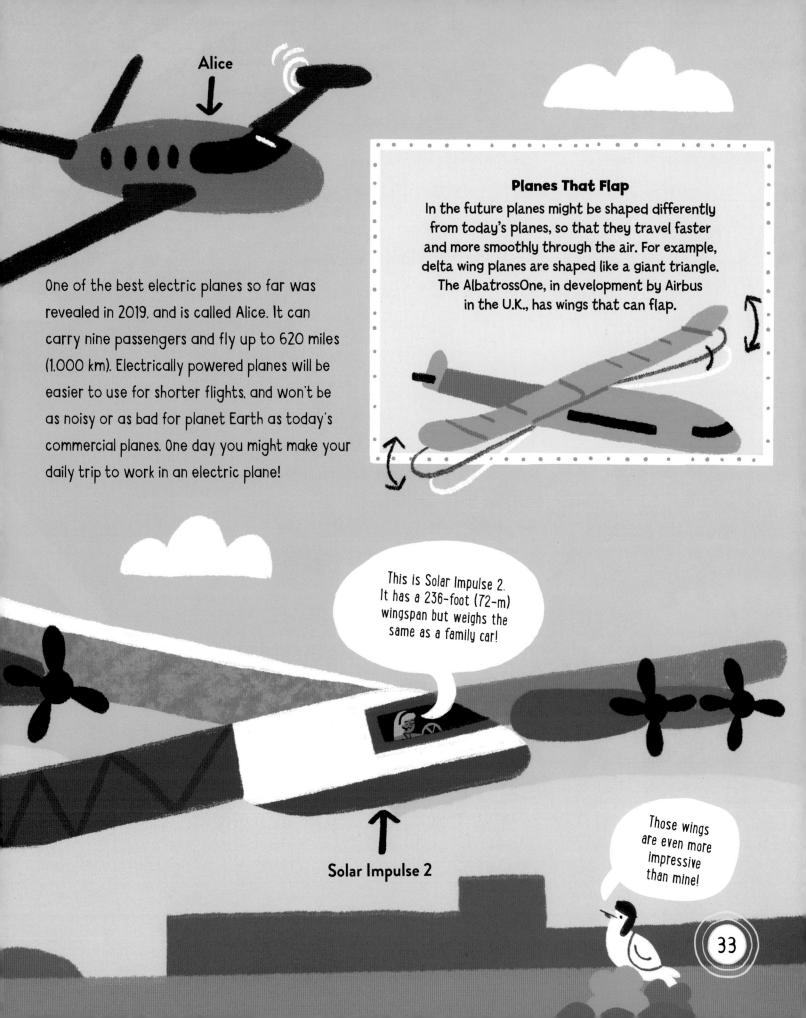

Alice

One of the best electric planes so far was revealed in 2019, and is called Alice. It can carry nine passengers and fly up to 620 miles (1,000 km). Electrically powered planes will be easier to use for shorter flights, and won't be as noisy or as bad for planet Earth as today's commercial planes. One day you might make your daily trip to work in an electric plane!

Planes That Flap

In the future planes might be shaped differently from today's planes, so that they travel faster and more smoothly through the air. For example, delta wing planes are shaped like a giant triangle. The AlbatrossOne, in development by Airbus in the U.K., has wings that can flap.

This is Solar Impulse 2. It has a 236-foot (72-m) wingspan but weighs the same as a family car!

Solar Impulse 2

Those wings are even more impressive than mine!

Helicopters

Helicopter wings are different from airplane wings, bird wings, and bat wings. These spinning rotary wings make helicopters amazing aerial acrobats.

The rotary wings mean that helicopters are extra clever. They can fly and land straight up or down, hover, fly backward and sideways as well as forward, and they don't need a runway.

Those wings are **weird**.

Most modern helicopters have a big main rotor and a smaller one at the back—this type of helicopter was designed by Igor Sikorsky and flew for the first time in 1939. They're not easy to fly.

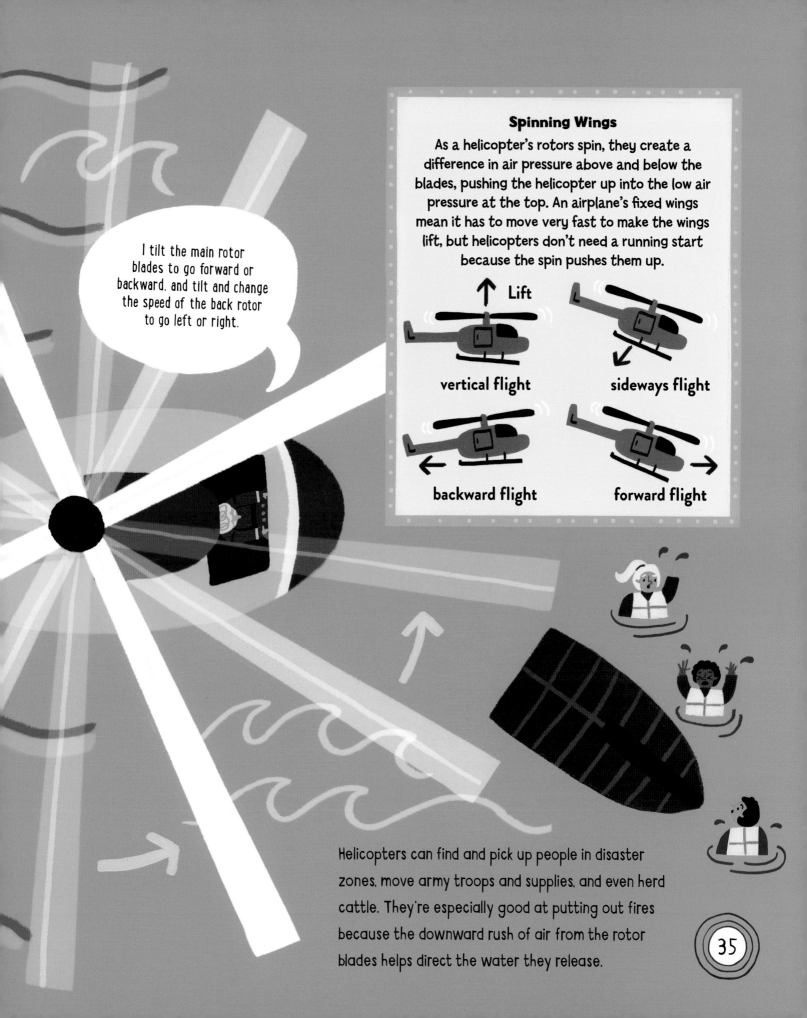

I tilt the main rotor blades to go forward or backward. and tilt and change the speed of the back rotor to go left or right.

Spinning Wings

As a helicopter's rotors spin, they create a difference in air pressure above and below the blades, pushing the helicopter up into the low air pressure at the top. An airplane's fixed wings mean it has to move very fast to make the wings lift, but helicopters don't need a running start because the spin pushes them up.

Lift

vertical flight

sideways flight

backward flight

forward flight

Helicopters can find and pick up people in disaster zones. move army troops and supplies. and even herd cattle. They're especially good at putting out fires because the downward rush of air from the rotor blades helps direct the water they release.

Wings in Space

Only this part of the shuttle is reusable. The two rocket boosters and the fuel tank are only used once.

Space rockets zoom out of the Earth's atmosphere without wings, but the world's first reusable spacecraft had wings so that it could fly back to Earth at supersonic speeds.

The Space Shuttle was the first reusable spacecraft. It whooshed into space with the help of huge rocket boosters, then returned to Earth and landed like a glider. It took satellites, astronauts, and probes into space, and traveled to and from the International Space Station, which is like a big science lab that orbits the Earth, and which the Space Shuttle helped to build.

Wingless Rockets

Wings are to help fly in air. Rockets are thrust up out of the air and into space as quickly as possible using enormous engines. There's no air in space, so they don't need wings.

There are other spacecraft with wings, like this one. One day, this kind of craft might take paying passengers into space. Maybe you'll take a trip to the Moon and back in one of them.

The shuttle had short wings. They didn't help with taking off or flying in space, but allowed the spacecraft to glide in to land at stomach-churning speeds far faster than the speed of sound. Because they couldn't take off, space shuttles sometimes took a piggyback ride on airplanes to get to launch sites!

Wings That Don't Fly

Some birds have wings but can't fly at all. Here are some of our flightless feathery friends.

Ostriches are the world's biggest birds.

Kiwis are in the same family group as ostriches, but we're only chicken-sized.

Kakapos and kiwis are nocturnal flightless birds that live in the forests of New Zealand. Kiwis' wings are only about 1 inch (2.5 cm) long and are completely hidden underneath the bird's feathers. Kakapos are a type of parrot—they can flap their wings but can't fly.

Penguins use their wings to propel them through water. The fastest-swimming penguin is the gentoo, which speeds along at up to 22 miles per hour (35 km/h).

We can be fierce and have been known to kill lions!

To make up for being too big and heavy to fly, ostriches can sprint on land at 45 miles per hour (70 km/h). They use their wings to slow down or help turn corners at high speed.

There aren't very many kakapos left since predators such as cats were brought to New Zealand.

Flightless Wings

There are a variety of reasons why flightless birds don't fly. Birds need wings big enough to lift the weight of their body—ostriches and other big birds got too big! Penguins adapted to swim rather than to fly millions of years ago, so their wings act more like flippers. For birds such as kiwis and kakapos, a lack of predators meant that flying wasn't so useful to them, and their wings gradually stopped being able to fly.

Sometimes gentoo penguins dive out of the water and whiz through the air—so we're sort of flying.

Balloons still fly today, mostly for fun. There are even balloons with glass bottoms for very brave passengers!

Blimps are lighter-than-air flyers too—they mostly use helium instead of hot air, and can carry more people.

You don't often see blimps—planes proved more popular.

I could fly faster than this!

Flying Without Wings

Some things can fly—or, at least, seem to fly—without any wings at all.

Hot air balloons fly because the hot air inside the balloon is lighter than the air outside. The first hot air balloon, designed by the Montgolfier brothers, took off in 1783 with a sheep, a duck, and a rooster on board!

Sugar gliders are adorable possums from Australia, Indonesia, and Papua New Guinea. They have a thin skin that stretches between their fore and hind legs, allowing them to glide 150 feet (45 m) or more between treetops. They can't really fly—it's more like controlled falling from one tree to another.

We love sugar, and get it from nectar, pollen, and tree sap, but we eat spiders and insects too.

We probably evolved this trick to escape from bigger fish who want to eat us.

Flying fish are found in warmer seas all over the world. They can't really fly either, but they look as though they can. They build up speed underwater—up to 37 miles per hour (60 km/h)—then launch into the air. Their large fins act like wings, allowing the fish to reach more than 3 feet (1 m) high and glide for up to 650 feet (200 m).

Wandering Albatross Wings

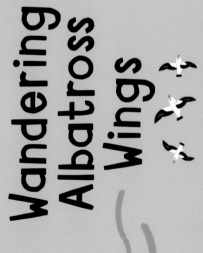

The wandering albatross has the most impressive wingspan of any bird in the world. These magnificent flyers can measure more than 10 feet (3 m) from wingtip to wingtip.

These huge birds spend most of their time soaring over the sea on the wind, seldom coming down to land. They've been recorded traveling an astonishing 75,000 miles (120,000 km) in one year as they fly around the Southern Ocean.

Aircraft engineers have been studying how albatrosses fly. These extraordinary birds are experts at energy-efficient flying, and could help make planes more efficient too.

Wandering albatrosses glide through the sky on air currents. They angle their huge wings into the wind to push them higher and higher, then swoop back down toward the ocean. They rarely have to flap their wings.

I eat fish, squid, and shellfish, and I can drink sea water, so I'm quite happy out at sea.

The birds land in big colonies once every two years, when it's breeding time. They are reunited with their partners—usually the same one throughout the birds' lifetime. Usually the female albatross lays just one egg, and the parents take turns looking after their chick.

There are more than 20 different kinds of albatross. Sadly, all of them are either endangered or likely to become endangered, mainly because the birds get caught in fishing lines. We can help them out by only buying fish that's caught using bird-friendly lines.

18 feet (5.5 m)

Biggest Ever Wings

The bird with the longest wingspan ever discovered was the giant teratorn, which lived until around 6 million years ago. Its wings measured 18 feet (5.5 m) across.

All Sorts of Birds

There are at least 10,000 different kinds of bird in the world, and there might be many more than that. They come in all sorts of colors, shapes, and sizes. Here are just a few of the world's amazing birds.

Peregrine falcons are the fastest-flying birds. They can reach 230 miles per hour (370 km/h) as they swoop down to catch their prey, which is as fast as a Formula One race car at top speed.

It sounds impossible, but common swifts can keep flying nonstop for ten whole months. They migrate from Europe to Africa for the winter, and some of them never stop throughout the entire journey. They fly up very high at dawn and dusk, and it's thought they have a nap as they gently descend.

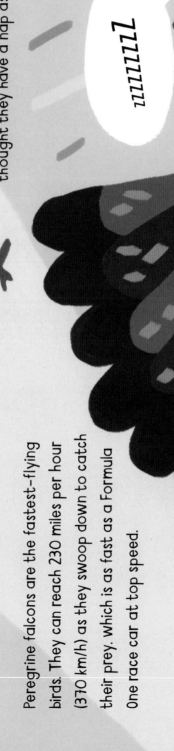

zzzzzzzZ

As well as being some of the cutest birds in the world, puffins are excellent swimmers. They can dive down to 200 feet (60 m) deep, flapping their wings to power themselves along and steering with their webbed feet. Unlike the wandering albatross, puffins flap their wings a lot when they fly—up to 400 times a minute.

The tiny male bee hummingbird is the world's smallest bird. At 2.2 inches (5.5 cm) long it's not much bigger than a bee, with a wingspan about the length of a grape. Like all hummingbirds it has to flap its wings super-fast to stay in the air.

My wings flap so fast it makes a humming sound—and that's why we're called hummingbirds.

We need to eat a lot of fish to give us enough energy for all that flapping.

Timeline

Climb aboard our super-fast time machine for a quick journey through the history of wings.

100s of million years ago (MYA)

Insects are the first creatures to fly on Earth.

11th century AD

Monk Eilmer of Malmesbury attempts flight with homemade wings.

1452–1519

Scientist and artist Leonardo da Vinci draws more than 100 designs for flying machines.

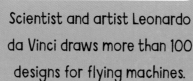

Around 400 BC

Kite flying in Ancient China takes off.

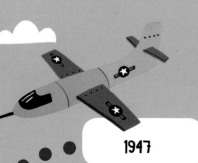

1947

Chuck Yeager flies the Bell X-1 rocket plane at supersonic speed.

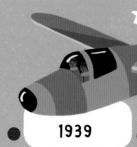

1939

The Heinkel 178, the world's first jet plane, flies.

1952

The first passenger jet plane goes into service.

1969

Supersonic passenger jet plane Concorde makes its first flight.

225 MYA

Flying reptiles called pterosaurs appear on the planet.

147 MYA

Archaeopteryx, a meat-eating feathered dinosaur that could flap for short distances, appears.

More than 2,000 years ago

The story of Icarus, the boy who flew too close to the Sun, was told in Ancient Greece.

70 MYA

Birds that looked more like modern birds arrive.

1783

The first hot air balloon, designed by the Montgolfier brothers, takes off.

1853

Inventor George Cayley builds the first successful glider.

1927

Charles Lindbergh is the first person to fly solo across the Atlantic nonstop.

1903

The Wright brothers make the world's first heavier-than-air powered flight.

1981

The first reusable space shuttle launches.

2016

Solar Impulse 2 makes the first around-the-world flight using solar power.

INDEX

Now you know all about wings. look out for a book about wheels!